MW01383770

Preparation for the Ultimate Purpose

IF I PERISH, LET ME PERISH, BUT I'M NEXT.

Dr. Angela L. Corprew-Boyd

This Book Belongs To:

_____

An ANOINTED WOMAN OF GOD
who is NEXT!

"And the king loved Esther above all the women,
and she obtained grace and favour in his sight
more than all the virgins; so that he set the royal
crown upon her head, and made her queen. . ."
Esther 2:17

PREPARATION FOR THE ULTIMATE PURPOSE

Manufactured in the United States of America.
ISBN: 0-9670909-1-1 EAN

Cover & Page Design: Dana Fuller
E-mail: fullerdesigns@yahoo.com
Cover Images Supplied with the Permission of Hermera.

Publisher: Dr. Angela L. Corprew-Boyd
Published by: Women Empowered in the Millennium, Inc.

ACKNOWLEDGMENTS

There are many people who have been an inspiration to me, so if I forget to put it on paper, I do thank you from the depths of my heart. My sincere gratitude to my pastoral colleagues for knowing that I could when I did not feel it, taste it, or want it. A special thanks to my family – Dad, Mom, brothers, and sisters – who have in their own way given words that thrust me to move one step forward to completing what God had already promised. To my friend Aretha Janine Olivarez: without you, your wisdom, and knowledge, how could I have completed it. You're the BEST!

DEDICATION

This book is dedicated first to God. I thank Him for the vision to pursue the call and the stamina, fortitude, faith, and peace of mind to complete it. To my God-given angels who never gave up in encouraging me when times of disappointment hovered over my life: Reggie and my three little joys (Devin Jared, Donovan Jaye, and Dawn Janae). Finally, to Amire Lily Harvin, you are somebody!

ENDORSEMENTS

"Women...are you seeking God for purpose, promise and destiny? Then this book is a must. From chapter to chapter, you will glean vital principles to prepare you for your destiny - that one thing in life only you can do. That one thing in life that only you are born to do...destiny! The story of Vashti and Esther take on new meaning in this anointed work."

Dr. Wanda A. Turner - Author, Teacher, Preacher
Inglewood, CA

"...*I'm Next!* is a unique, refreshing approach to the study of Esther. Written in a practical manner, Dr. Boyd guides you through the process of what matters most. If you long to know who you really are inside with a confidence that transcends any title bestowed upon you or that means more than your present condition of existence, then read on and prepare to have your hope restored that you have a unique destiny waiting to be fulfilled."

Rev. Dr. William D. Tyree, III
Pastor of First Baptist Church, Berkley
Norfolk, VA

"I was anxious to see what would happen in the next chapter. It was as if I was playing the role of Esther in my mind - maybe because I had been in the 'if I perish' position before. This book gives women the courage to step up, and step out. Thank you for being in the birthing room with us."

Aretha Janine Olivarez- Author
Orlando, Florida

"Dr. Boyd, in this work, opens a door of prophetic understanding that has been closed for a long time. Her biblical insight and ability moves the reader to a greater level of understanding to the Word of God. Her ability to braid the Word of God with practical application gives the reader a clear insight to the unfolding drama that God is directing in their lives. As Esther was NEXT, the reader will ask Dr. Boyd what is NEXT?"

Rev. Lamont D. Brown
Pastor of Mt. Olive Baptist Church
Virginia Beach, VA

"An owner's manual for fulfilling one's purpose."

Ress Walker - Teacher
Virginia Beach, VA

TABLE OF CONTENTS

"But as it is written, eye hath not seen, nor ear heard, neither have entered into the heart of man, the things which God hath prepared for them that love him. But God hath revealed them unto us by his Spirit..."

1 Corinthians 2:9-10a

INTRODUCTION

Have you ever been in a place and felt all alone, depressed, empty and out of place? I've been there and have not understood exactly what God was doing. Have you ever felt you were born into the wrong family, lived in the wrong neighborhood, went to the wrong school, married the wrong man, attended the wrong church, and you have been dealt the wrong hand? I've been there and have constantly asked God, "What's wrong with me?" While seeking God, I have found out that everything I have done, every place I have been, every person I have met, and every experience I have come through was in preparation of my ultimate purpose: to bring glory to God!

I was pensively pondering my childhood one day when God spoke to me about a little girl. I began to reflect on where I had been and what God had allowed me to experience. God began to put things in perspective for me. Isaiah 55:8 ignited my spirit, *"For my thoughts are not your thoughts, neither are your ways my ways, saith the Lord."* There was a message in that for me. It wasn't my choice but God's choice, and I must accept the plan He had predestined for my purpose. In other words, this was a story which would be told; a story of overcoming the odds of a child who some thought wouldn't make it. Why? Because I came from a neighborhood that wasn't ritzy. I rode in a car that wasn't fancy. I wore clothes that weren't designer.

But, I had one thing that no one could take away—the hope of Jesus to make ME a STAR!

Growing up in a family of ten, I was the eighth child and the sixth girl. It was a challenge, but I survived. How? God sent anointed men and women to my rescue, helping me to understand who He had created in me and the purpose that He had predestined for my life. I called these men and women my "midwives." When I was pregnant in the spirit, they would call and encourage me to push. When I was depressed and lost in myself, they would call and tell me to push. When people in the church had hurt me to the point that I wanted to run to the wilderness like Elijah and sit under the juniper tree, I would hear the voice of one of my midwives saying, "Push, Angie, just push!" I did not realize that God had appointed every one of them to my life until later. They would be a part of my story.

One day, I was reading the book of Esther, and God spoke to me: "I'm going to make you a STAR." I was excited, but there was a process that I had to endure to receive my promotion. There were some struggles that I had to endure to get my crown. There were some storms that I would have to weather to reign as the queen. There were some enemies I had to love if I would be called to center stage. Was I ready to accept my reward?

God prepared me by sending me midwives. When you read the book of Esther, you will find the STAR; Esther, didn't do it by herself, but God used Mordecai as her midwife. Little did I know or understand why Argie Lamb, Barbara Duers, Essie Davis, Pat Selden-Black, Marionette Butts, Delores Eure, Charles Brabble, Dwight Parker, Minnie Blount, and Eunice Woods had been sent to cover me during my years of schooling. But, God knew what He was making, and He used them to help me. Thank God for my midwives; they were angels in disguise helping me to become a STAR in the eyes of God.

"For promotion cometh neither from the east,
nor from the west, nor from the south.
But God is the judge: he putteth down one,
and sitteth up another."

Psalm 75:6-7

CHAPTER 1

Move: You're In My Place

God, in His infinite wisdom, knows why you were created. He speaks in Psalm 139:15-16 (NIV), *"For you created my inmost being; you knit me together in my mother's womb. I praise you because I am fearfully and wonderfully made; your works are wonderful, I know that full well. My frame was not hidden from you when I was made in the secret place. When I was woven together in the depths of the earth, your eyes saw my unformed body. All the days ordained for me were written in your book before one of them came to be."* He knew you before you were formed in your mother's womb. This truth allows you to recognize that your purpose was established before God created you. This means God created you for that specific purpose. When God is ready for you to walk in your purpose, He sets up the process for you to endure and journey through with grace. For He never allows you to enter a place without first endowing you with what you need to come up and out. Look at Luke 4:1; the Spirit of God filled Jesus with the Holy Spirit after His baptism and led Him into the wilderness, the valley. God endowed Him with power; Dunamis, the Comforter, the Intercessor, the Paraclete, the third personality of the Trinity – the Holy Spirit, in order to be successful with His purpose. His purpose on earth was twofold: (a) to preach the Gospel and (b) to heal. Although He endured hardship, struggle, and persecution; He came out as pure gold and accomplished His task because He had been given what He needed to come out of where He was led. This leads to the truth that God creates specific, tailor-made situations just for you to walk in your purpose. Let's look at the story of Esther where many have found themselves today.

Esther was not born into the lower class of society. She was the child of noble Jewish parents; however, she was orphaned at an early age, and grew up on the outskirts of town. But, God knew the plan for Esther. He had already predestined a midwife in the name of Mordecai just so that the purpose for which He had created would come into fruition. He used Mordecai, her cousin, as the overseer of a purpose that would save the nation. How did Esther's ultimate purpose become unveiled? When it's time for your purpose to be revealed, God will create a situation just for that very reason. You never know who God is going to move out to move you into position. Vashti, the queen of Persia, was in place, but God knew her purpose as Queen had come to an end; there He created a situation that would prepare the next Queen.

Vashti was a woman of integrity, a woman of character, a woman who chose not to insult the God she served for anyone. She was asked by her drunken husband King Ahasuerus to dance or parade around other men who had come to the palace to feast, drink, and be merry. As the queen, it was her responsibility to be submissive to her husband the King.

It's important to note here that you should not jeopardize your anointing with God or insult Him by degrading your character or walking outside of your purpose. Don't try to please your pastor, your husband, or anyone else for that matter by doing anything that would cause you to be demoralized in the face of the people you must serve. Don't be a "yes-girl" just because you think the pastor holds a position in the church or in his or her heart for you. Don't operate on your emotions when you know it's not the right thing to do. Your integrity is what's at stake. When your integrity is gone, what else do you have? How do you serve the people of God? Who can trust you? Who can have faith in you? Don't lose what you have for man's promotion. For in Psalm 75:6-7, we read, *"For promotion cometh neither from the east, nor from the west, nor from the south. But God is the judge: he putteth down one, and sitteth up another."* Wait for God to create the right condition at the right time for the right position in the right place. When you wait on the Lord, you can have the assurance that you're next in line for a miracle. Just wait!

Vashti decided she would no longer be insulted, used, or put on the spot for position sake. You have to be like that, ladies. Take a stand, and wait for God. All you have is your integrity. Don't compromise it. When Vashti refused to dance before the King and his "boys," God's plan went into action. While the enemy thought he was dethroning the queen, God had a greater plan for the one who would save the coming King…Jesus Christ. Esther's ultimate purpose was about to be fulfilled. She was NEXT!

When Vashti was ruled unfit to be the queen of Persia because of her disobedience to her husband the King, a decree went out; and she was dethroned. When you refuse the king's proposal and the one who you thought chose you for the position, expect him to dethrone you because you are not fulfilling the purpose for which he placed you in the position. By now, you have recognized who you serve instead of who placed you there. You have come to the realization that for God you live and for God you die; from here on, all the in between will and shall be pleasing in the sight of God. Make up in your mind that you will not serve man, but you will serve

God. When you do this, you must declare that this is the day that the Lord has made, and you can rejoice and be glad in it because you're next in line for a miracle. Just wait!

Vashti was no longer the queen; therefore, someone had to take her place. It's time for you to take someone's place. You have been waiting on the Lord. You have been in constant prayer. You have been faithful in your position. You have been *"steadfast, unmovable, always abounding in the work of the Lord, forasmuch as ye know that your labour is not in vain in the Lord"* (1 Corinthians 15:58). Because of that, God is about to elevate you. Are you ready for the promotion? Just wait!

"....and be not conformed to this world: but be ye

transformed by the renewing of your mind,

that ye may prove what is that good,

and acceptable, and perfect, will of God."

Romans 12:2

CHAPTER 2

Reformed: Transformation in Process

If you are going to be next, your mind has to be transformed by the Holy Spirit of God. To be transformed is to be changed, rehabilitated, converted, improved, and or renewed. You are not the same! You leave the old and begin anew. Your past has to be wiped from your mind because God has already forgiven you of your past. As a matter of fact, He chooses not to remember it; *"I will forgive their iniquity, and I will remember their sin no more"* (Jeremiah 31:34c). If you are to accept the elevation, you must have a renewed and transformed mind. You must rid yourself of those things that hinder you by going to God. If you allow it to fester in your spirit, it contaminates your inner parts. And once your inner parts (spirit + soul = inner man) are contaminated, all of who you are is affected. STOP it before it happens. Be loosed from your past by praying, reading your word, and staying in worship with God. Make another declaration; Philippians 3:13 reads, *"Brethren, I count not myself to have apprehended: but this one thing I do, forgetting those things which are behind, and reaching forth unto those things which are before,…"* Let the devil know that you are reaching for your predestined elevation by being transformed by God. If Esther could do it with her sorted past, you can too.

From the poor house to the palace, Hadassah was on her way! Hadassah was Esther's Jewish name. Poor, outcast, marred, and easily forgotten by the rest of society, but not by God. Who would have ever thought she would rise to the top. Because Mordecia was in the right place at the right time, serving in the palace, he was one of the recipients of the good news: a beauty contest for the selection of the new queen. Without hesitation, he entered Hadassah, his orphaned cousin, into the beauty contest. It does not matter what your past is or where you have journeyed in your life; your past does not hinder your purpose. You may have experienced an abusive relationship, a drug infested neighborhood, an alcoholic parent who did not nurture you, or an unwed mother who did not want you. Your past does not stop God from using you for his glory. You simply have to want to be used and not be choosy about who He appoints to help you.

God had already given Mordecia the plan. Her name must be changed to conceal her true identity. That's just like God. Sometimes He has to change your name, conceal your true identity, or erase your past from other's minds before you can be used in the Kingdom. In 1 Corinthians 1:27, we read, *"…but God has chosen the foolish things of the world to confound the wise."* When God is moving to transform you, allow Him to have His way even if it means leaving the familiar to go to the unfamiliar. God has it all in control.

Hadassah's name was changed to Esther,

meaning STAR! Mordecia escorted her to the palace; immediately, she found favor with the chambermaids. When God is ready to elevate you to your place of destiny, believe me, favor is already opening doors that no man can shut. She was welcomed in the palace because God predestined it. When God opens the door for promotion, no devil in hell can stop it but you! This is a lesson for you to learn. Stop dwelling on the past, and press forward. Isaiah 43:18 tells you, *"Remember ye not the former things, neither consider the things of old."* It's behind you; get over it. In 2 Timothy 1:6, we read, *"Wherefore I put thee in remembrance that thou stir up the gift of God, which is in thee by the putting on of my hands."* God has given you something even greater – your gifts; they will make room for you in the kingdom. Esther operated on that scripture by walking in her purpose.

Esther did not have time to dwell on what could have happened to her as a child or why she was left without parents. This helps you to recognize that you can't contemplate why these things you have experienced are a part of your past; *"all things work together for good to them who love the Lord"* (Romans 8:28). It would be her past that God would use to elevate her for His glory. Everyone needs credentials to qualify for God. Some may be in pursuit of pleasing God with their education, their big house, or their fancy car; God, in His infinite wisdom, qualifies the called instead of calling the qualified. When you try to qualify yourself with education, wealth, and position; you are really disqualifying yourself in the eyes of God. In Matthew 6:33, Jesus said, *"seek ye first the kingdom of God and its righteousness and all these other things will be added unto you."*

Your challenge is to recognize that *"if any man be in Christ, he is a new creature: old things are passed away; behold, all things are become new"* (2 Corinthians 5:17). You may need to know how to become new. Even though you have accepted Christ, there are still some fragments of your past haunting you, tormenting you, or dwelling in your spirit. Every time you think you have gotten past it and are ready to go to the next level, there is something that triggers its memory. It's a trick of the enemy. You must use the power that God has given you to speak against the past and the enemy who tries to hinder you. Begin to speak positive thoughts and resist the enemy, and he shall flee. Use the word that has sustained you and proven true in your life. Don't allow the enemy to win because you are NEXT!

Esther was in the palace. It was time for her outward transformation because God had already done a work on the inside. The very thought of her being inside the palace and accepting Mordecia's plan which God had given him lets you know that God had already changed her inner being. You must have an inner transformation before the outward transformation occurs.

"But who may abide the day of his coming?
And who shall stand when he appeareth? For he is
like a refiner's fire, and like fuller's soap: And he
shall sit as a refiner and purifier of silver: and he
shall purify the sons of Levi, and purge them as gold
and silver, that they may offer unto the Lord an
offering in righteousness."

Malachi 3:2-3

CHAPTER 3

Refined: I'm Next

Once Esther was inside the palace, the work of preparation began; however, it did not happen over night. When God calls you to be NEXT, there is a process that you must go through. There is a plan that God has tailor-made just for you, and you are the only one who can fulfill the requirements of the plan. When God calls you, He calls you by name; when God calls you, He calls you into His presence; when God calls you, He calls you when you least expect it. When God calls you, He prepares and equips you for the call. When He does that, the process of preparation is not a choice of your plan but obedience to His plan.

In the plan of God, the process is specified for you. When He is ready to do a quick work, as in the example of Esther, sometimes there is a three-step process that He will accelerate. That three-step process has an integral catalyst, which is **PREPARATION**. Preparation centers on the following steps: **SANCTIFICATION, CONSECRATION, and MEDIATION**. Esther mastered all three.

First, as God did with Esther, He must sanctify (separate) your pain from your purpose. God took Esther from a very difficult situation. He separated her from her parents, her home, and even other orphan friends that she may have had while she was on the outskirts of town. These were people that she would have trusted and depended upon just to survive. When God is ready to use you in an awesome way, He separates you from people and things that are not ultimately a part of your purpose. He may take away old friends and acquaintances or tell you to leave your country, your kindred, and your father's house just as He did Abram. But, just as God had something greater in store for Abram and Esther, He has something great in store for you if you obey. Are you willing to obey God and leave everything?

You may be in a situation right now that is causing you pain and hindering your purpose. God will create a situation just so you can see His hand move suddenly in your life. He will take you to a place of isolation where there are no inhabitants just to get your attention. You may lose your friends; you may lose your job; you may even lose a relationship; but you will never lose God. Although you may be in a place of emptiness, void, and rejection, it's the place God wants you to be for this season. It's the place where you really find out who God is in your life. It's the place where you can worship Him in spirit and truth because He has separated you from mundane situations, irrelevant conversations, and the insignificant problems that face you daily. He wants you to trust Him if you are to be NEXT! He says in 2 Corinthians 6:17, *"wherefore come out from among them, and be ye separate, saith the Lord and touch not the unclean thing: and I will receive you."* God is waiting to receive you from things that have hindered you and held you back. Your mind has to be willing to be refined and elevated to the point that God can use you if you allow Him.

If you are to be NEXT, separation must occur; however, there is also **consecration**. Esther was consecrated. Yes, God sent Esther to the palace to consecrate her. If you have been called by God, He must be the one who consecrates you. To be consecrated is to be given rights and privileges. It was this very assignment that became fulfilled in Esther's life. Being consecrated meant being blessed and approved for what God had called her to do – reign as queen. When Esther was received in the palace, the Bible tells us she pleased Hegai, the keeper of women, and was given the choice place to live. When God is consecrating you for your assignment, there will be some choice people and places He has already set up to receive you. All you have to do is be obedient. Your obedience will expedite your reward. The Bible tells us that Esther's kindness pleased Hegai, and he speedily gave her things for purification. Likewise, your kindness and well-doing is about to be rewarded!

Finally, there is **mediation**. No matter how much you have been separated or consecrated, the work only becomes real through the mediator who is God.

Your sanctification may be different from others. Your consecration may be different from others. But, God has already designated those who shall assist in escorting you to your place of destiny. If

God has called you to preach, teach, prophesy or lay hands on the sick, preparation means spending time with God. It also means studying to show yourself approved unto God and not man. If God wants to prepare you through seminary, go. However, you should continue to be faithful and submissive to the leadership that has authority over you. In order to prepare, broaden your knowledge. Begin to seek God for wisdom that you may know the deep things of Him. While you are waiting for your ultimate purpose to be unveiled, don't lie dormant; rather, stay in the word, and allow God to speak to and through you. With all of Esther's PREPARATION, her purpose was complete after a year. One year Esther was in the palace being sanctified and consecrated through the authority of her mediator,

God the father. It was preparation that allowed her to use wisdom for her ultimate purpose. God was preparing her *"for such a time as this."*

You must realize that when God appoints you for the completion of any assignment, it's about His getting the glory. As He prepares you, remember to whom you belong and who gave the promotion. Even when Esther seemed a bit confused, God continued to use Mordecia, her midwife, to help her push. Mordecia had to bring to her remembrance the real reason for her promotion. You must never forget how you got to where you are. Never forget who putteth down one to sitteth up another. It is God who is in control and makes things happen. When you were an orphan, a drug addict, a prostitute, a whoremonger, a liar, a fornicator, or an adulterer and saw no grace, He *"made grace abound toward you, because he is able"* (2 Corinthians 9:8).

God chose you to be refined in the refiner's fire. Accept the process, and go through with pleasure because His grace is sufficient for you. His strength is made perfect in weakness. Yes, there comes a time when you may feel like giving up while you're waiting; but, don't. God has not left you nor has He forsaken you. He is simply developing you while you wait in line to be NEXT! Esther's preparation took a year; yours may take longer. But, in the midst of being prepared, count it all joy; you shall receive your just reward for having the patience to endure your cross.

"To every thing there is a season,

and a time to every purpose under heaven…"

Ecclesiastes 3:1

CHAPTER 4

Released: It's My Season

I believe Esther realized before it was too late that God had appointed her for something far greater than just being the queen. With all the storms she encountered in her life and the trials she may have conquered, there had to be a reward. When you see God taking you through and bringing you out, you must realize that He is developing you for something great. I Peter 4:12 reads, *"Beloved, think it not strange concerning the fiery trial which is to try you, as though some strange thing happened unto you: But rejoice, inasmuch as ye are partakers of Christ's sufferings; that when his glory*

shall be revealed, ye may be glad also with exceeding joy." I believe that Esther recognized that if she was going to reign with Christ, she had to suffer for Him. If it had not been for her decision to go see the King, you could ask, 'what would have happened to the Jews? Would the annihilation have taken place?' In any event, it would have been an incident with potentially catastrophic consequences had she not gone to see the king. And remember, Jesus the Christ, the Messiah, was Himself a Jew. What an assignment from God Esther had! Can He trust you to be bold like Esther?

If so, you can declare that it's your season, your season to accept God's plan for your assignment. I'm sure when the King sent out a decree for a new queen, more than virgins showed up. That did not stop Esther from being entered in the beauty contest by Mordecia. He knew God's plan and was making sure it would be fulfilled. Don't become discouraged if you see the entire kingdom show up for the job you believe God has promised you. Don't become dismayed if the position in the church has already been filled. Don't be alarmed if you know you are not qualified for the job. Don't lose hope because you know your education and skills don't add up to what is being requested. Rest assured that if you keep Philippians 1:6 in your heart *"Being confident of this very thing, that he which hath begun a good work in you will perform it until the day of Jesus Christ,"* it shall come to pass. Esther saw that there were women coming from all over the provinces to enter that beauty contest; however, she was still confident. Even though some were from wealthy families; she was still confident. Some were from homes with two parents; but, she was still confident. Some had been in the palace with the king; but, she was still confident. Some already had what she needed from the maidens; but, she was still confident. Some had even been told that the position belonged to them; but, she was still confident. Esther *"calleth those things which be not as though they were"* (Romans 4:17b). Esther spoke her own destiny as it was predestined by God.

When you begin to think of your inadequacies, your frailties, and your inferiorities, you give way to the enemy and doubt what God has already spoken. When a call goes out from the King, everyone wants to be the NEXT one. Many were called and some called themselves, but only one would be chosen. The fact that the one who was called had been sanctified and consecrated gave great preparation for the position. Women came for the position and the prestige; but, they were not willing to pay the price that would have to be paid. When you accept the assignment, don't just look at the position and the prestige; you may have to pay a price. However, if you know the assignment has been designed for you by God, then you will also know that you are the redeemed of the Lord. He has already paid it all just for you.

Have you proclaimed that this is your season, and you're NEXT! No matter what it takes, who is in line, and how many might show up; it is up to you to decree, YOU'RE NEXT. Don't let this season pass without you walking in your destiny. God has released you for such a time as this.

" . . . O my Father, if it be possible,

let this cup pass from me: nevertheless

not as I will, but as thou wilt."

Matthew 26:39

CHAPTER 5

Esther: A Model for 21st Century Women

God's hand of providence and protection on behalf of His people is evident throughout the book of Esther. The book of Esther was written with a twofold purpose: (a) to unveil how the Jewish people were protected and preserved by the gracious hand of God from the threat of destruction and (b) so that women of God can observe how Esther is a model for 21st century women. When you dissect the story in its entirety, you see God's plan to save the Jews and how Esther was the chosen one just as Christ was chosen for you.

Esther was chosen by God to be a model for 21st century women. As a woman, you may identify with Esther's character, personality, or situation in spite of your profession, title, ethnicity, or religious preference. Needless to say, Esther is found, even if only a fragment, in women of this world today. As Christ was chosen to be the sacrificial lamb of the world, you find the Christ in Esther. In Genesis 1:26 (KJV), we read about when God created man: *"let us make man in our image, after our likeness..."* When God created Esther, He made her in the image and likeness of Himself and His son; Christ was in her. As a woman of God, you can identify with her character because you too were created in the image of God and His son.

Esther, like Christ, put herself in the place of

death for her people but received the approval of the king. She also portrayed Christ's work as advocate on your behalf. Esther's story unveiled a demonic threat to annihilate the people of God; thus destroying the messianic line, the King of Kings, Jesus the Christ. However, God's plan is at work, and He always prevails. How is God's plan at work in your life today? If you take an in-depth look at Esther, the character, you will find the answer. Esther modeled three important ideals that will allow you to see yourself as she was placed in position for her ultimate purpose. They are (a) the will of God, (b) the way of God, and (c) the work of God.

Esther modeled **the will of God.** In modeling the will of God, you must be humble, obedient, and willing to do what God has called you to do. In spite of any opposition, you must be ready to move when God says to move. As she modeled the will of God, you see her as humble, obedient, and willing. She was **humbled** by her orphaned experience. She found herself abased after being born into a noble Jewish family who had been carried into captivity when Nebuchadnezzar was reigning as King. Esther did not allow her condition of being an orphan to stop her. In spite of her situation, she was **obedient**. When her cousin Mordecai entered her into the beauty contest, she did not refuse because of her condition. She accepted and obeyed his leadership. When Mordecia came to her with the devastating news about the plot of Haman, her obedience to his plea prevailed once again, in spite of her position as Queen. If you are to be in position for the ultimate purpose and destiny of your life to be fulfilled, then you must be willing to forsake all, even your position, to allow the plan or the will of God to come into fruition. The will of God is your **willingness** to accept what He has planned no matter who the messenger, what your past may be, or where you are in your problem. Sometimes you must go against political power, tradition, family, and familiarity in order for God's will to be done in your life. Whatever God plans for you to endure, you must have an accepting spirit or a willing mind to say yes to His will. Esther's willingness to obey Mordecia with a humble, obedient, and willing spirit led to her preparation of the ultimate purpose God had predestined for her life. If you are to be NEXT, you must model these attributes even in the midst of adversity, just as Esther did, and allow Christ to be seen in you. As you see the Christ in her, remember what Jesus said in Matthew 26:39, *"And he went a little farther, and fell on his face, and prayed saying, 'O my Father, if it be possible, let this cup pass from me: nevertheless not as I will, but as thou wilt.'"*

Secondly, Esther modeled **the way of God.** In modeling the way of God, you must see Esther's independence. In her independence, she was courageous and wise and had a sincere belief in the power of prayer. Although Mordecai was her midwife and trained her in the way she should go, she was still an independent woman when the ultimate decision had to be made. Her wisdom led her to instruct Mordecia on what to do. He was to gather the Jews together and hold a fast on her behalf. Clearly, she had an extremely fervent belief in prayer. Esther was deeply distressed when she heard of the plot against the Jews. In wisdom, she considered what God wanted for such a time as this. She allowed the word to work for her so she *"committed her **way** unto the Lord; trusted in him; and he brought it to pass"* (Psalm 37:5). She, once again, would not allow her position as Queen to prevail over God's plan. For we read in Proverbs 19:21 (RSV), *"Many are the plans in the mind of a man, but it is the purpose of the Lord that will be established."* Esther, by modeling the way of God, represents the dreams, hopes, and ambitions of women who are ready to be prepared for their ultimate purposes for which God has already predestined, for them to be NEXT!

Finally, Esther modeled **the work of God.** God has called women to the forefront to complete a great work. Whether it is in your home, your church, or the work place, God has a work for women to complete. If the work of God is to be fulfilled, you must model Esther's confidence and character. From the time she was orphaned to the time she was presented in the contest, from the time she received favor from Hegia to the time she is selected as Queen, she modeled these virtues. A great deal of preparation were part of God's plan so that the work of God could be completed. In her preparation, Esther was confident that she had been prepared to fulfill her destiny. For we read in Philippians 1:6, *"Being confident of this very thing, that he which hath begun a good work in you will perform it until the day of Jesus Christ."* Esther was assured; she was secure; she was certain; there was no doubt in her mind that she had been chosen for something great. When Esther realized that it was time for God's work to be done, that her purpose would be part of the completion of God's plan, she forgot about herself and began to concentrate on the one who sent her to the throne. Here you see the character of Esther come alive. God chose her because she was trustworthy, respected, and responsible. Ladies, if you are to be NEXT, you must model Esther's character.

Her character exemplifies several ideals. She was

trustworthy, respected, and responsible. Those are the reasons God will choose you for your specific purposes. He knew that Esther could be trusted for such an awesome task: to save a nation. He knew that when the final trumpet sounded, He was not at all concerned about the decision she would make, because He could trust her to fulfill the prophecy and complete the work He had chosen for her to do. Esther was respected. Before she was selected as queen, God had already bestowed favor upon her. That favor translates into respect. Her status in society had nothing to do with respect. Her position in society had nothing to do with respect. It had everything to do with the plan of God for her life and her purpose being complete. Esther realized that in order to receive respect, she must model it. Her courteous and polite demeanor was acknowledged in the palace. She was appreciative of the maidens of Hegai as well as her cousin Mordecia. She was tolerant of her year's preparation and was patient in allowing the work of God to be done in her life. Esther was respected as a woman of God because she respected others. Furthermore, Esther was definitely blessed in her preparation with responsibility. To be responsible, you are accountable. If the work of God is to come to completion, then you must be responsible. Esther's responsibility meant she was held accountable for the work of the Lord. To be accountable is to utilize the knowledge God has given you for all situations. When Esther was distressed about the news from Mordecia of

Haman's plan, she did not panic. She thought before she acted and considered the consequences of all who would be affected. She was reliable as well as accountable. She accepted responsibility for being in the position and, in turn, set an excellent example for those women who would aspire to be like her. She modeled the work of God for 21st century women when it comes to character. Ladies, if you are to model the work of God, you must exemplify the character of God; and He will choose you to be NEXT!

Certainly, the story of Esther challenges 21st century women. She modeled the will, the way, and the work of God; helping women recognize where they need to be for promotion. She exemplifies housewives, mothers, pastors, ministers, professionals in the work place, and so many more. If you take a closer look into the life of Esther, you will find yourself. When you do, ask God to prepare you as He did Esther for the completion of your predestined purpose. Do not allow fear to grip you, for the work of the Lord must be complete in your life.

"For God hath not given us the spirit of fear; but of power, and of love, and of a sound mind."

2 Timothy 1:7

CHAPTER 6
CONCLUSION

Having a spirit of fear is a stronghold that many have to overcome. Esther was fearful when Mordecai came to her about the decree for all Jews to be killed. She sent a response to Mordecia, but it was not what he wanted to hear (Esther 4:8-14). Little did Esther know at that time that it was her ultimate purpose to be in the position as the queen. It was a set-up from God. From her being orphaned to her entering the beauty contest to her receiving favor from Hegai, the keeper of the women, to her being chosen as the queen, God's plan was being fulfilled through Esther for the coming of the

Messiah. When the enemy, Satan, the oppressor, the prince of the air realizes how important your purpose is to God and those who will be loosed because of your obedience, he is angry. He begins to scheme and set traps that will cause you to fall. He begins to play with your mind. He sets up a plan himself to come and kill, steal, and destroy the very fight you have left to overcome. Look at what Esther did; she sent word to Mordecia to pray and fast— not just for anything or anybody—for her. When you are in a situation where fear tries to overcome your spirit, pray and fast. God will speak and open doors even while you are contemplating what you must do.

God's plan for your life is already in action. He wants you to recognize who He is and what He has already done so that you will seize the moment in His timing to be NEXT!

If you are ready to walk in your ultimate purpose, pray this prayer: *Dear Lord, your humble servant, (say your name), comes before you to give thanks for the blessings that have already been bestowed. I thank you for allowing me to step out of the clutches of fear and into faith. I thank you for allowing my spirit to be opened to your will. I thank you for transforming me, refining me, and releasing me to the next level. I thank you for enlarging my territory and preparing me to walk with boldness to the place you have already predestined with my name on it. I speak right now to every mountain, to every circumstance, to every problem, to every enemy, and to every stronghold that shall present itself as a weapon, knowing that it shall not prosper. I recognize who I am and the power in me to overcome. Lord God, as I make myself available to you for your glory to be revealed, I praise you in advance for the souls in my family, my church, my community, and on my job who will be saved because of how you used me for such a time as this. Thank you for trusting me to be NEXT! This is my prayer. AMEN.*

ABOUT THE AUTHOR

Angela Corprew-Boyd has always been one to set her mind on things hoped for; knowing that with faith, God is able to make all things happen. As she grew up, the eighth child of ten, she didn't allow the negative statistics spoken in her spirit to hinder her from pursuing her destiny. At an early age, she realized that she was gifted and chosen by God to influence a nation of hurting, depressed, and oppressed men and women. Understanding what a mighty seed she was carrying, she allowed God to anoint and appoint her to do His will. Her motto is Philippians 1:6 which reads, *"Being confident of this very thing, that he which hath begun a good work in you will perform it until the day of Jesus Christ."*

With a passion to see and assist God's people to walk in their purpose, she has an anointed fervor to teach and preach the unadulterated truths of God's word. Praying that they will embrace what will escort them to their destiny, her desire is that men and women separate their pain from their predestined purpose while *"forgetting those things which are behind, and reaching forth unto those things which are before"* (Philippians 3:13b). Angela aims to impress upon all humanity the need to unmask who they think they are and confront the real life issues trying to destroy them from fulfilling their dreams. In her pursuit of purpose, the Lord led her to follow her own predestined purpose according to His will for her life. God established for her the ministry that He placed in her spirit. She is the founder of Women Empowered in the Millennium Inc., a ministry aiming to meet the needs of the "whole" man and woman and the issues he/she faces through intercessory prayer, workshops, seminars, Bible studies, and conferences. She is also the founder of Angela Corprew-Boyd Ministries, Inc., a ministry assisting men and women who have been called to leadership in the Body of Christ. God has opened doors for her to travel to Africa, London, the Hampton Roads area, and other states to preach the gospel. She also acts as a conference consultant and speaker.

The Lord has afforded Dr. Corprew-Boyd the opportunity to pursue higher education. She received her bachelor of science degree in English with a minor in Speech from Old Dominion University in Norfolk, Virginia. God continued to allow her to pursue her education and attain her master's degree from Norfolk State University in Urban Education/Administration and Personnel Management. She also received her Certificate of Advanced Graduate Studies from Regent University in Virginia Beach, VA. She pressed on to earn her doctoral degree in Strategic Leadership from Regent University. At the present time, she is employed with Chesapeake Public Schools as an Assistant Principal at Crestwood Middle School. She has served as an instructor and the Chief Operating Officer of the School of Ministry where the founder and president is Dr. Ronnie D. Joyner, Pastor of Philadelphia Fellowship. Dr. Boyd was ordained as an Elder in the gospel ministry. Since her ordination, God appointed her to the staff at First Baptist Church, Berkley in Norfolk, Virginia as the Assistant to the

Pastor, Rev. Dr. William D. Tyree, III.

Dr. Corprew-Boyd is married to Reginald, and they are the proud parents of three children: Devin Jared, Donovan Jaye, and Dawn Janae. She wants people to know that everything that she has accomplished professionally, educationally, and spiritually is because of what God has predestined for her life. She has accepted it and has walked in His will for it. God gets the glory and the honor for it all. She has opened her heart, mind, and soul and has made herself an empty vessel, waiting patiently to be used by God.

Women Empowered in the Millennium, Inc. &
Angela L. Corprew-Boyd Ministries, Inc.

VISION

To meet the needs of the "whole" man and woman and the issues he/she faces, through workshops, seminars, conferences, intercessory prayer and Bible Study, while pursuing his/her predestined destiny. Also to aid these anointed men and women to develop, enhance, and empower their leadership abilities to effectively serve in the Body of Christ.

Women Empowered in the Millennium Inc. and Angela L. Corprew-Boyd Ministries, Inc. have been anointed, appointed, and assigned by God to empower men and women of diverse cultures, religious denominations, and educational backgrounds who are ready to embrace their purpose and destiny. The ministry offers an anointed transfer that brings about change in the "willing heart" of all whom are present. If you are ready to reach another level in God through the power of this ministry, we want to serve you in your next conference, workshop, convention, etc.

- Leadership Training Seminars
- Kingdom Building with special emphasis in Ministry Enhancement
- Organizing and structuring seminars, workshops, and conference, etc.
- Articles of Incorporation and 501(c) (3)
- Skills of a servant (Armor bearer)
- Christian Education

- Church Administration
- Develop a Christian leadership style
- Develop a commitment to God
- Discover Spiritual Gifts
- Develop, nurture, and cultivate Spiritual Gifts
- Develop a commitment to the ministry
- Develop the characteristics of an Empowered Leader
- Various workshops and seminars to meet the needs of men, women, and youth

"We're on the Edge of Time"

To contact the author, write:

Dr. Angela L. Corprew-Boyd

Women Empowered in the

Millennium, Inc.

505 Waters Road

Chesapeake, VA 23322

Visit our website at

www.angieboydministries.org.

womenempowered98@aol.com